Another Look At

FAKENHAM

A look at the town
in the first thirty
years of this century

Jim Baldwin

With poems by
Ellen Van Damme

A NEW CENTURY

Fakenham in 1900 was a typical Market town in an agricultural environment. However, unlike most others it also had quite a substantial industrial undertaking with the printing works of Miller Son & Co employing some 200 persons, nearly 10 per cent of the population. The town was also well supplied with Railway Stations (two), Schools, Mills, Public Houses, a Gas Works and Churches, the newest of which was the Roman Catholic Church of St Anthony of Padua, completed in 1910.

So what was life like in those days? As always it is best reflected in the newspapers of the time, in this instance the Eastern Daily Press and the Dereham and Fakenham Times.

In April of 1903 a meeting was held in the Corn Hall by the Fakenham Free Church Council to protest about the "intolerable injustice" of the Education Act to Non Conformists. It seems that the appointment of School Governors with a ratio of two Church of England to one Non Conformist did not suit them at all. The same month saw a letter from Arthur Stebbings complaining about the smell of gas in the Church during evening service.

Nellie Miller, daughter of printer Thomas Miller Jr, was the subject of a presentation at her father's Wharfedale printing works in respect of her impending marriage to Mr R. Owen Goddard who was private secretary to Lord Hastings. Thomas Miller lived at Wensum House, Hempton and on the way from the Church at Fakenham after the wedding 80 girls from the printing works lined the roadside and threw flowers in the path of the couple. The reception was held in a large marquee with the Town Band in attendance in the evening.

The paper then printed a list of who had given what as a wedding present!!

A letter to the paper that month entitled "Old Fakenham" recalls that one of the shops in the long since demolished (sic) block of buildings at the East end of Norwich Street (in front of the site of Town Sign) was a grocery business belonging to a Mr Bacon.

In October of that year there were complaints about the way that the Salvation Army were going about their business.

The Corps had been formed in 1883 and had fitted out the "Star" barn in Oak Street which they hired from a Mr Strangleman, and they were still based there when they fell foul of the local populace on Saturdays and Sundays.

It seems that, at 10-30 in the evenings (closing time) they would march, band playing, through the town, not only disturbing those who were the worse for drink but also those who were sober and asleep in bed.

On Easter Monday 1908 the foundation stones of the Buckenham Memorial (Primitive Methodist) chapel were laid with the help of the Rev. Henry Buckenham's widow. Henry Buckenham was a Fakenham man who had undertaken two expeditions to Africa for the Methodist movement on one of which he died.

Thomas John Miller Sr, founder with his son and family of Miller Son & Co, died in May 1908 aged 87. The firm eventually became the Fakenham Press and closed in 1982.

It could be said that these were the times where "Old Fakenham" and the "New Fakenham" merged. On the one hand there were horses, wells, gaslights and "Honeycarts" whilst on the other hand there were the beginnings of those things that we take so much for granted today.

By the end of 1914 the town Sewer was working, pumping from Hall Staithe up to the farm on Creake Road. Then there followed the Telephone with an exchange being opened in a yard off the East side of Bridge Street. In 1932 the East Anglian Electricity Supply Co established itself followed in 1938 by piped water.

People had more time to themselves and were able to patronise local concerts or perhaps dance to one of several local dance bands such as the Versatile Five or Leslie Feakes' Syncopated. You could buy yourself a Wireless set from Whites Wireless in Upper Market or Bennetts, and you could run it with an accumulator purchased and regularly charged by Gilbert Dugdale from Stibbard who opened a shop near the Telephone Exchange.

The town's first Cinema opened its doors after the Military had vacated the TA Drill Hall in Holt Road; later, the Electric Pavilion opened in the former school in Norwich Road while a third, the Central, made use of the old Corn Exchange from 1932 until recent times.

But perhaps the thing which changed the face of Fakenham most was the Motor Car. At first it was a novelty, the First World War made it acceptable and Henry Ford and his contemporaries made it available. Later in this book we will look at some of the businesses set up to service the automobiles but it didn't stop there. Two oil depots were set up near Fakenham East station to store and distribute petrol brought in by train. One still remains.

Roads had to be made more suitable, indeed there soon followed some changes to the town plan. One of the most significant was the emergence of Malthouse and Greenway Lanes as roads, they later became known as the "Bypass". Allied to this was the demolition of several cottages at the junction of these lanes and Wells Road including the "Heater" cottages (so called because their shape was akin to that of an iron) and the Pound cottages. The motor car was not the sole reason for their demise. Social conscience created new laws to deal with bad housing and the same laws were responsible for the building of council housing estates, in this instance Jubilee Avenue where the occupants were re-housed.

Another change to the social life of the town was in the education field. Both the British and National school buildings were in some need of attention by the turn of this century although the former had been rebuilt only a few years earlier after a fire. A new school was built in Queen's Road in 1912 to house both C of E and Non Conformist children although girls and boys were separated.

Highfield House was built by the Campbell family in 1820 and just over a century later it became a Secondary school, complete with a Campbell ghost!

But some of the older ways lingered on, the horse in particular. In 1933 there were still three Blacksmiths working in Fakenham, George & Balls in Oak Street, Herbert Peircy in Nelson Road and James Wakefield in Quaker Lane whose blacksmith father Lavender Waters Wakefield was so called because he was reputed to have been a sweet smelling baby!

Life was getting better, but not for long. The Depression and War were on the horizon so let's pause and take ANOTHER LOOK AT FAKENHAM.

THE GREAT FLOOD

Heavy winter rains or spring thaws often cause the water table to rise on the meadows around the river Wensum at Fakenham. Indeed, in recent years the river burst its banks and sheep had to be rescued from the meadows by boat.

However nothing has yet surpassed the great flood of 1912. On the morning of August 6th a "low" over the North Sea set off a violent storm over Norfolk. By 9 a.m. the following day 7·5 inches of rain had fallen and the Wensum valley, in particular Norwich, became a disaster area.

Some idea of the ferocity of the storm can be gathered from the picture on this page. Probably taken from the Gas Works it shows the river by the M & GN (Fakenham West) station with Hempton Mill in the background. Because the trees were in full leaf many succumbed to the wind and some of the largest trees in the town fell victims of this tempest.

Hall Staithe, then a residential area, was the only place of any note in Fakenham where households were inundated and a boat from a boathouse there was used to ferry supplies to the inhabitants cut off by the water as can be seen in the top picture.

The river bank was not high enough to contain the water along by the Hempton road as the bottom picture shows. The horse and cart make it, while the children paddle and the cyclists wonder whether or not to attempt to go further.

As the floods subsided the wall around the Fakenham Mill pool had to be breached to allow the flood water to drain away, while further north at Barsham a railway bridge collapsed with a goods train on it thus cutting for a while one of the town's two rail links.

FIRES

By the turn of this century Fakenham's Parish Fire Brigade had been in existence for some 20 years and for most of this time the superintendent had been Mr Richardson from the Bell Inn. However he gave up his post in 1903 as a result, it seems, over a dispute regarding the ladder.

On Thursday February 2nd, 1908 the brigade attended their biggest ever fire when Joseph Baker's house and shop in Norwich Street caught fire and was destroyed.

Looking like a still from a Benny Hill TV show the top picture shows firemen in action damping down what was left of Joseph Baker's property, while the bottom picture shows the brigade in action again, this time in Queen's Road. There, in 1913, a fire destroyed buildings opposite the newly opened school luckily without damage to it.

T. J. Miller Jr, was an amateur photographer who took a number of pictures of these fires. It seemed, however, that he was reluctant to photograph his Wharfedale Printing Works when it burned down on Saturday 21st November, 1914. The picture of the boys having a "garwp" at the wrecked printing presses was taken by someone else.

It is said that, at the height of the fire, molten type metal flowed down Whitehorse Street where the factory was situated.

THE TOWN BAND

At the time of writing Fakenham Town Band has just entered its second century having been formed in 1882.

The idea had come from a meeting at the Crown Inn in October the previous year when a committee was formed with a Mr Holt as secretary. Also involved was Martin Bambridge, the town's first sub-postmaster.

After much canvassing the necessary finance was obtained and thirteen young men were duly formed into what was known as a Temperance Band. This may strike the reader as rather amusing since the band was formed in a public house and then proceeded to practice in one, The Bell. However, perhaps because of this, in 1885 it became Fakenham Town Band, a name it has retained ever since.

Eight years later things were going well enough for a programme for re-equipment to be undertaken and so new instruments and uniforms were purchased. One change in the uniform was the abolition of the "Pill Box" hat which was replaced by a more modern peaked cap. Little is known about the new instruments but we do know that the band owned a portable bandstand.

For some reasons now lost in history the fortunes of the band began to decline. Attendances by musicians slowly dropped off and by the early 1900s the membership was down to a mere handful of players,

certainly not enough to undertake any engagements, so, in 1907, the Fakenham Town Band folded up.

The problem remained as to what to do with all the equipment and this was solved when the Parish Council took over the trusteeship of the band, putting the instruments into store in case the band should ever rise again. The bandstand also came into their care, to be hired out as required.

After a while interest in the Town Band increased and a new band was formed. It was some while before it made any public appearances and its first was for the funeral day of King Edward VII when they marched from Barons Hall Lawn sports field to the Market Place, where our photo shows them arriving heading the Yeomanry, the Infantry (under Capt Powell) and the Cyclists (under Capt D. Dewing).

After surviving the First World War the band found itself doing very nicely thank you. Fakenham had its own competitions where bands would march through the town to Barons Hall Lawn (second photo), passing on the way adjudicators listening behind closed shutters en route. The home band seems to have done well in these as well as other competitions as far afield as London.

It was during this period that one of Fakenham's colourful characters enters the scene – his name was Tommy Ruffles. Tommy like many other bandsmen had his roots in the Salvation Army band, and he joined the Town Band in 1916 where he became one of the prominent members of the Junior Section. Soon he was in the main band and at the same time was running a dance band called the Snappytones, and, as if this wasn't enough, there was a time when he also played for the Reepham Band.

Eventually Tommy Ruffles became Bandmaster, a post he held until his death in 1957.

9

THE GREAT WAR

Great Britain was the only nation to declare war on Germany in 1914.

In Fakenham horses were requisitioned, reservists were called up and young men were encouraged to join up and fight the "Wicked Hun".

There was little physical change to the town though. A TA drill hall had been built in Holt Road, another wooden building was constructed in Wells Road and troops were billeted in the old barn off Oak Street where Cromwell had once slept.

The drill hall eventually became a cinema, then a roller skating rink and is now the workshop of a tractor dealer. Another tractor dealer also uses the old barn in Oak Street, while further down in Wells Road the wooden hut was turned into shops including the Wells Road Sub Post Office which remained there until they were demolished a few years ago.

While there was little physical change there was certainly a great change to the population. The picture of the Square shows the Fakenham Detachment of "C" squadron the Norfolk Yeomanry receiving the Blessing on Friday August 4th.

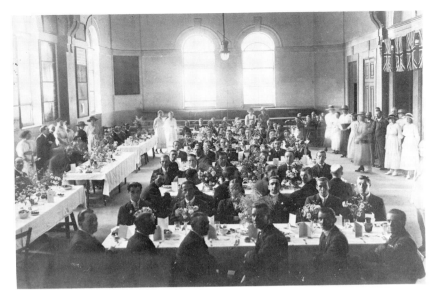

It is not known to this writer how many local men went to the war. Fakenham's population was about 2500 at that time, and it is not impossible for there to have been 2 out of a family average of 5 fighting for their country. There were 80 that did not come back and for many others life would never be the same again.

For those that did come back there was dinner waiting in the Corn Hall (now the Central Bingo Club) and later, in the early days of peace, the proud members of the British Legion lined up at Fakenham East station to welcome Admiral Earl Beatty when he visited the town.

FAKENHAM'S BUSINESSES

When the Dereham & Fakenham Times celebrated its centenary in 1981, R. W. Newman, who had been in business for 110 years, were proud of the fact that they had placed an advert on the front page of the first issue. There are several other businesses in the town today who can boast a similar longevity of trading. Powells the saddler going back to 1820, Parker the jeweller and W. J. Aldiss both going back to the 1890s, Moores the baker, Duffy & Sons, Stead & Simpson, the Universal Suppliers (formerly Joseph Baker), Richardsons and Long & Beck all dating back to about the same time.

Stewardsons were in business as printers and stationers in the early years of the last century and probably before. They finally ceased printing in the 1960s and are now absorbed into Aldiss store. It was George Stewardson who, in 1860, got permission to extend his shop over the top of the Lych Gate in Upper Market.

There were many other businesses with a very long lifetime although their names are not familiar to today's generations. Tucks were well known for their tasty bread for many years, baked in their shop in Wells Road, shown in this photograph. Adjoining was the Cattle Market Tavern public house, so called because of its proximity to the old Pig Market. At the end of the street can be seen the former Pound Cottages, the Pound itself having been built in the wrong place so that the builder was obliged to demolish it and start again!

The Readwin family were traders and builders for over 120 years. In 1797 one of them drew the well known picture of the "old" Barons Hall and the family name was still over a shop in Bridge Street at the outbreak of the First World War.

The Wright family were in business during the middle of the last century and by the end of that century there were no less than 10 branches of the family trading in the town, many of them in competition with each other as boot and shoe repairers.

A similar situation existed with the Utting family although their trades were more diverse.

Many old photographs of the Market Place show the Bowles' shops. Clara Bowles had hers on the east side of Bridge Street facing the Market Place while, later, Henry traded from the other side of the street where the Bank now stands. This family traded for over 50 years.

The father of Sir Robert Seppings (1767 to 1840), one time surveyor of the Navy, was a cattle dealer, although not a very good one it seems. The family name still shows up in the business world in the early 1900s, although they would have been descendants of Sir Robert's uncles as he had no surviving sons himself. At one time the family owned the Dukes Head public house in what is now Cross Quaker Lane (at that time Chapel Green) and were brewers in property nearby.

Without doubt, the oldest business in the town was Sheringham and Overman whose premises in Holt Road have recently been converted into a Supermarket. Previously the company had traded from the Market Square and could trace their beginnings back to 1657 when Edmund Peckover moved to the town. At one time the Peckover family had an interest of some sort in most of the property in the old town area. They also had many business interests including a wine shop on the site of the Off Licence in Oak Street. At that time part of the property fronted Hall Staithe where there was a brewery. This was later run by Charltons until it was demolished in 1912 to make way for the sewer pumping station.

The Peckovers died out in 1836, but their Bank continued as Barclays and what remained of their other interests became Sheringham and Overman.

There were many other names that bring back memories to older Fakenham residents. Drewell's, Bone's, Elliot's, Heyhoe Miller's, and there are some who found that their names had become unofficial place names. Leach's Corner is where the town sign stands. It was once the site of Leach's shop. Wainwright's Corner is where Norwich Street and Bridge Street meet, and our picture shows Cecil Wainwright standing outside the shop that his father Joseph had opened in 1875. It lasted nearly 100 years.

13

Down Memory Lane

What a fascinating thing is one's memory,
What hundreds of things come to mind,
So let's stroll down Norwich Street in Fakenham
And see what delights we can find.

Let's call in at Newman's for hair-cut,
At Chapman P.D. for some meat,
At R. Bone for watches and E. Bone for bikes,
They're all there in old Norwich Street.

There is hardware and guns too at Baker's,
At Pooley's fine groceries and beer,
While W. J. Aldiss will show you
His clothes and his finest footwear.

At Priest's you'll find stationery and newsprint,
And Stark's will supply flowers and seeds,
And Wainwright's just there on the corner
Is just bursting with musicians' needs.

Then when you have finished your strolling,
Though there's quite a lot more you could see,
You can just step into the "Chocolate Box"
Where they'll serve you a nice cup of tea.

Two views of commercial Fakenham. The east end of the Market Place well before 1900 showing the town pump to advantage. Note the key over the Ironmonger's shop. This remained there after the business had moved!

The other picture on this page is Norwich Street just prior to the First World War. The drum clock dated back to 1856 and was lit by gas.

THE MOTORING SCENE

It is not certain who had the first car in Fakenham, but we know that Cecil Wainwright from the Music Shop was amongst the pioneers. However there were soon plenty of cars in the area and by 1913 the town had its first motoring mishap on the Sculthorpe road as the picture opposite shows.

Baxters were the first motor engineers in the town, establishing themselves in 1890 in Holt Road where they remained until recent years. Southgates, a firm of coachmakers who had been established in Oak Street since 1825, soon followed and in 1914 they became Ford dealers, as can be seen below, and remain so today as R. C. Edmondson.

"Pom" Blake returned from First World War service in the RFC ("Germans? lovely fellows, shot me down you know") to open up as a motor engineer in Wells Road. For a while he was mechanic to racing driver Tim Birkin and at the time of his death in 1979, was still in the process of rebuilding one of his cars (it can be seen in the Bygones collection at Holkham).

George Howard, "Pom's" partner, split from him and went to Quaker Lane where he catered for the growing interest in Motorcycling, Fakenham having its own club.

John Whites had a similar business near what was then the new Co-op in Norwich Road. After its closure in the 1920s it was taken over by Robert Carley. Later he demolished the original buildings shown in the middle photo opposite.

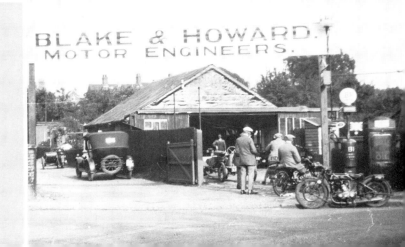

SPORTING LIFE

In 1815 a Fakenham/Hempton/Walsingham cricket team were all out for nil in a match against a Brisley/Dunham/Litcham side. This may account for the fact that we hear no more of a cricket team in Fakenham until 1883 when it is believed that the town team was formed! It soon established itself on its home ground of Barons Hall Lawn in what was then Station Road.

Loaning this ground from them after their formation a couple of years later was the town football team, The Ghosts. There were of course, other football teams in the town. For instance there was for many years a Wednesday team, made up of those who worked in shops etc and were free on early closing day. The printing works of Miller Son & Co also had quite a useful team named after their factory, the Wharfedale Works. This picture shows them to advantage during the 1910 season. The lad sitting front right is the late "Chum" Medlar, a good all round sportsman and like others probably played for more than one team.

For the more sedate there was the Lion Bowls Club, dating back to the early 1800s. Taken in 1900 this picture features T. J. Miller Jr in the centre front, with a beard.

There was Tennis, Golf on Hempton Green, later moving to the Racecourse and racing itself at the course which moved from East Winch to Pudding Norton in 1906. One of the men who moved it, Harry Gates, actually put his wedding day back a couple of days so that it did not clash with the first meeting on April 16th.

However, if you were looking for something quieter you could always go boating on the river Wensum.

ROUND AND ABOUT

Although not a Fakenham man, Sir George Edwards, founder of the Agricultural Workers Union, spent his last years in the town living in Queen's Road opposite the playing field that he campaigned for and near to the cemetery where he now rests.

The picture on this page shows him proudly holding the union banner. Behind him is the late Ken Doy who devoted his life to the town, its people and Methodism.

Billy Cole was a character who lived in a little cottage near the bridge in Hall Staithe. He was the town's political cartoonist of a sort, especially if he thought he could get a laugh at someone's expense. In the case of the cartoon on the next page it was the Chairman of the Parish Council. The old brewery was almost next door to Billy.

The country scene in the middle picture is in fact a view of the remaining part of the "old" Barons Hall and barn from Norwich Road, probably in the 1930s. The old hall was built in 1593 and demolished in 1812 when the new hall was built nearby, except for the wing shown here. This lasted until the 1970s but the barn still remains.

The old Wesleyan Chapel features in the picture at the foot of the page. At the time of the Methodist Union the congregation (reluctantly) crossed the road and joined with the Primitives, turning over their building to the Salvation Army who remained there until it was bombed in 1941.

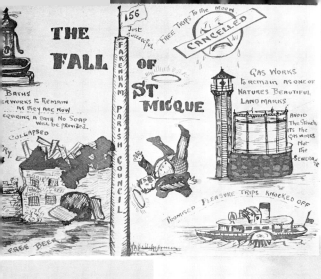

THE FALL OF ST MICQUE

156 Just Successful

FREE TRIPS TO THE MOON CANCELLED

FAKENHAM PARISH COUNCIL

BATHS
ER WORKS TO REMAIN
AS THEY ARE NOW
EQUIRING A BATH NO SOAP
WILL BE PROVIDED.

COLLAPSED

FREE BEER

GAS WORKS
TO REMAIN AS ONE OF
NATURES BEAUTIFUL
LAND MARKS.

AVOID
THE STENCH
ITS THE
GAS WORKS
NOT THE
SEWERAGE

PROMISED PLEASURE TRIPS KNOCKED OFF

A Fakenham Hospital has never materialised in spite of money raised by Hospital Weeks. This Carnival procession was part of 1920s Hospital Week, passing along Oak Street.

And, ending Another Look At Fakenham, an interior shot of the Parish Church of SS Peter & Paul taken in 1914.

Epilogue

Upon the Wensum's northern side
The town of Fakenham stands,
Church tower looking down with pride
O'er town and pleasant lands.

There have been changes through the years,
We've lost the trains and stations,
And much that's old can still be found
With orders of preservation.

The mills and maltings are no more,
The brick kilns all are empty,
But though we still have several pubs
At one time there were twenty.

Old names have vanished with the years
And new ones ta'en their places,
But the town itself is just the same,
A town with friendly faces.

The Thursday market's grown with time,
But cattle you'll not find there,
Still corn-hall auctions draw the crowds
And Long and Beck preside there.

The town has spread its arms most ways,
It welcomes all and sundry,
For friendships here for young and old
On weekdays and on Sundays.

The publishers would like to
thank the following for their
help in the production of
this book.

Kevin Baldwin *(back cover illustration)*
Carley Motors *(photo page 17)*
Fakenham Camera Club
Fakenham Local History Society
Mrs. C. Wainwright *(photo page 14)*

This Page: Fakenham Mill.
Front Cover: Fakenham Church & Grove House.
Back Cover: Tunn Street.

© Jim Baldwin Publishing
ISBN 0 9509060 1 8
Published by Jim Baldwin Publishing,
Fakenham, Norfolk NR21 8LQ
Distributed to the trade by Paper-Klip,
Fakenham, Norfolk NR21 9AG
Typeset by Fakenham Photosetting Ltd.
Reproduced by Colourplan and
printed by Colourprint

A product of Fakenham